How to Tell

If He's Alcoholic:

An Excerpt From the book

Does He Drink Too Much?

We received many requests for copies of this chapter separately. You asked for it, Ladies—and here it is.

By Beth Copeland, M.A., LMHC

Readers of "The Drinker's Woman" and of "How to Tell . . ." requested that I print the checklist in this chapter separately that we've done it. I was enlightened to that it was less expensive (! for both you and me !) and would be easier handled if it were bound like a book. Then other advisors explained that the reader of the checklist needed much of the material in the larger chapter. And I agreed. So, here you have the outcome: "How to Tell if He's Alcoholic."

"The need for change

bulldozed a road down

the center of my mind."

By--Maya Angelou

Chapter 5

Where you
  find out whether he has a real problem
  if so, find out how far it has progressed
  and find more food for thought

Wanna Know How Bad
His Drinking Problem Really Is?

Ever wonder if he's "a real alcoholic"? Wanna know for sure?

And if he has a problem, would you like to know just how bad it really is?

If you answer "yes" to both these questions, this is the chapter for you. It gives you answers, lots of 'em. And the checklist in this chapter is sufficiently comprehensive to convince everyone else too—even him—of what you will be able to see so clearly. Ready? Let's get to it!

*　*　*

About the Checklist

The chapters up to now will have covered the basics of over-drinking and the physical body and over-drinking damage to that body, most specifically the brain. Also covered are understanding his behavior, and the things he says. Most importantly, however, we've begun looking closely at what his behavior has been doing to you.

(Note: That explanation refers to the chapters previous to this Chapter 5 in the book "Does He Drink Too Much?" I tell you this so if you have more questions than are answered in this brief chapter, you can go to the full book containing much more information, information to help you understand what's going on with him, and how to better cope with it.)

We already can say with confidence that he definitely has a disorder. We can say that because you've become frustrated and desperate enough to pick up this book. And I can say it too—because you are desperate enough to pick up this book! Women whose men aren't over-drinking and causing problems aren't in the book shelves looking for info on him and what he's doing. By the time a drinker's woman is reaching out for help she's been pushed to her limits—else why reach out for help? She's about run through all her own resources and ideas—to no avail.

The strongest point made that pretty much pins down a diagnosis of a drinking problem is because his drinking and things associated with it are disrupting his life—and he doesn't change! I can assure that by now he had tried more than once to stop, or at least cut down. And those attempts have failed.

Second point: His drinking and the behavior it produces in him is disrupting your life, someone he claims to love, but he doesn't change. Yes, he's told you, likely by now, several times that he's quitting, or cutting down. And he meant well. Probably. But his attempts failed.

Worse: He cannot stop drinking the elixir that is slowly eating away his brain. Alcohol is toxic, it is a poison that destroys body cells (of special note it destroys brain cells, a condition that produces his changing behavior and thinking. It damages, then destroys his liver cells, kidney cells, esophagus cells and stomach lining.

Alcohol goes directly into the blood; you don't have to get it into your stomach for it to begin circulating; it goes right through your skin cells. Your blood is pumped through your body at many miles per hour, with force, and as soon as it leaves your heart and lungs (numbers 1 and 2 for survival, it rushes to number 3, your brain. It hits and begins damaging the cells it touches first in the part of his brain that is supposed to see that something is going wrong with his body and mind and behavior. (Nerve cells-brain cells are extremely delicate; alcohol acts like an abrasive, a light acid on delicate cells. They are injured, holes eaten in their cell skins, then their internal fluid leaks out, then its internal parts can't work anymore because they require the fluid to move around inside the cell, and the cell by then is useless. And it begins dying. Once it dies, it won't grow back.)

The screwy thinking, bad behavior, and most all the other stuff you see in him that you hate are the result. The Bad News is that at some point in the ongoing brain cell destruction caused by alcohol, he will lose the brain power to stop.

And especially, to stay stopped.

He is helpless at times, sick at times, dense and stupid at times. All this is due to failing body parts, in particular his brain.

You've seen by now that his worsening behavior and your worsening relationship problems are both directly connected to his drinking. But you're still not sure how bad his problem really is. Most people are leery of saying someone is a full-out alcoholic. (It would be interesting to do research and find out where that thinking is rooted. It's something akin to his freedom that he and most people think gives him permission to do this.)

So—to the upcoming checklist: If you're concerned enough about his drinking to have procured this book, have come this far, I can pretty much guarantee that he, indeed, has a problem. And if it is causing problems in his life and yours, the problem is by now well advanced.

The checklist is going to show you how bad his problem is, and what stage he's in. That's valuable information for you because it points you to your best approach; otherwise, you might be trying this and that until you run out of emotional steam.

Or are you there already?

This same checklist as well will pinpoint the best treatment that will have any hope of success. To date, I know of no treatment approach that has incorporated this simple tool in their assessment processes, nor have any incorporated them (or any like them) into their formal treatment plans—for which they are ideally suited.

The dilemma for most women hooked up with a man who drinks too much is not feeling "authorized" to diagnose him. Along with other problems this causes, the worst is what she should to cope, and to save herself.

The checklist consists of the *numerous* signs of a drinking problem. Yes, I know, most such checklists give you ten, maybe twenty signs—which practice has left all of you who will finally read this book still without solid, reliable information. The list of signs of a diagnosable drinking problem focuses on things (events and behaviors) that you've observed, and things you didn't directly observe but know about.

Your work here benefits you by giving you a good idea about what you actually are dealing with, which likely will be an eye-opener. You also get a strong affirmation of what your common sense has been telling you.

You'll also be in a better position to know what you need (or want) to do about your situation when you get a better idea of how bad his problem actually is now, at what point he is, and what comes next.

If he's in the Early Stage, there's some hope of recovery. But in the more progressed stages (beyond Late-Early Stage), the chances of getting effective help to change are practically nil. That's the Bad News here.

On the other hand, it's also Very Good News if it takes away forever your doubt and sense of guilt, the sense that you ought to be doing something to fix all this, that you *must* fix all this, that you're supposed to do something to fix all this.

Don't dread finding out here that he may be in real trouble; finding that out is really Good News for you. First, he's in this shape due to his own doing; second, you begin to understand just why life has been so difficult lately. And, likely, for some time. If you don't pinpoint what's really wrong, what's happening to him, you could spend the rest of your life feeling guilty and inadequate because you haven't fixed it.

The Bad News is that you can't fix this—not him, not the things he does so long as he drinks anything alcoholic at all. But while it can be Bad News about his true condition, for your sake, it's really Good News! You've been right! You now have both feet on the ground to begin determining your next best steps.

Knowing whether or not he's already beyond the stage where he's most likely to change, where change has a chance, can free you, which is Very Good News. Should he be at or beyond that point, and once you truly accept that, you finally have permission to stop trying to herd him and his behavior like a sheep dog, trying to "fix" him and the things he causes, trying to foresee what problems he can create, and trying to block him.

If he is at or beyond Mid-Early Stage, your attempts are pretty much useless (as many of you already know). In fact, your efforts are less than useless; your machinations are actually harmful—to you).

Just think: You will be able to dispense with all obsessing. That's because you will realize he has reached the level of brain deterioration where all your attempts at corrective action are useless anyway. (So what will you do with all that spare time?)

Knowing and understanding why he's extremely unlikely to accept any help or reach out for it, or stick with it should he reach out, you can relax. Again, because you will realize that his behavior and thinking changes are beyond your level of intervention. And what will you do with all the time this is going to free up for you? Hm-m—perhaps you can get a life!

Holding a solid assessment of his true condition, you don't have to be frustrated ever again. That's because you know in advance that most attempts for a good outcome are going to fail before you bother to set them up. Once he's much beyond this early stage, you will see (on the checklist) that you cannot expect much at all good to come from this man on the path he's taken.

Disappointment and frustration are the result of having plans, being emotionally invested in the planned outcome, and having it busted up. If he's beyond Early Stage, you can start reading books or seeing a counselor to help you back off and leave him to his self-destruction—while you protect your own interests.

You also need to know if he's already beyond the point where he's likely to go for help, and more importantly, for it to help him beyond the short term.

More Bad News that can be Good News is that he is almost sure never again to be the guy you fell in love with. Even if he is one of the fewer than 10 percent my research shows are making the turn-around and keeping it up. Brain cells that structured his personality back then have been altered. Brain cells die once injured (especially by the abrasive effect of alcohol, which draws out all the fluid from cells—which fluid is necessary for the cell to survive). And brain cells do not grow back.

Even if we find a way in the future to grow back dead brain cells, they would not still have the memories or thoughts or skills or personality. They would be blank. I tell you this because most drinkers's women live with a vague sense that one day he'll get all right and go back to being the guy you fell in love with.

It won't happen. For a very, very few—a portion of the some 10 percent of over-drinkers who pull out at all—hold onto or recapture a few of their good qualities, but not enough to be what they once were. No more than an athlete can come back from a severe alcohol problem and regain all of his strengths.

Alcohol doesn't only kill brain cells (which are just nerve cells); it kills nerve cells all over the body, and nerve cells not only perceive heat, cold, and touch,

8

they also trigger and control all muscles of the body. (That's why, with a degenerative nerve disease, a person loses control of his body. The nerves controlling a given body part are destroyed. Making them "drunk" causes the muscles to be out of control, which causes slurring, staggering, and loss of bladder control. And worse.

Knowing that he's beyond the point where your efforts will do much good seems to be a terrible thing but that knowledge ends up setting you free. You know in advance y our attempts won't work, and with more reading, you understand why.

You are clear-headed about what's really happening and which "battles" you have a chance to win and for which of them you may as well save your energy.

Most drinkers's women often feel strongly that they want to separate; if this is you, know that there are—at this moment—millions of women in the US along at the same crossroad, weighing the same painful and difficult decision. Whether you decide to stay with him or separate, understanding what has really happened will free you from much of the fear of having made a mistake. You'll make your decision based on careful consideration of what is best for you. Sacrificing yourself on the altar of "saving him" is a waste of a beautiful soul—you.

Only when a soldier leaves the area where the hidden explosives are can he even begin to heal his mental injuries, so are you. Do not expect yourself to remain in the status quo and finally get control, even of yourself. The problem at the heart of all your problems will prevent having enough clear-headedness and emotional stability to heal.

And do not discount the amount of damage you are likely suffering, the emotional and mental wounds that living with a man who drinks too much can inflict on his woman.

*　*　*

More Benefits of This Work

You'll also shed your own special kind of denial (the kind you share with 20 or 30 million other women in the United States alone, and with countless millions of others around the world). You and most all drinkers's women practice a form of partial denial. Denial is a mental trick we play on ourselves, insisting on seeing something in a way that makes us most comfortable, discarding anything which suggests otherwise.

It boils down to being unable to accept something you thoroughly dislike—for instance, that he is as hopeless as your observations tell you.

(A part of you knows he's beyond fixing, but a bigger part still believes that if you love him enough, as in Belle and the Beast, you will awaken him from his condition, a reversal of another fairy tale, Snow White).

Psychological "denial" also works to mentally shut out (or minimize in value or effect) something that threatens to overwhelm you.

Psychological denial isn't a bad thing. Wired in by the Manufacturer as a survival tool, denial is a reflex action your brain takes to protect you (itself) when events become too big for your current resources to cope with. Don't think you've been "stupid" or mentally deficient for being in denial. For sure, it has helped you survive to now; it has kept you from being overwhelmed by how truly bad your situation may have become.

Your subconscious, amidst its billions of other processes, also keeps tabs on your minute-by-minute levels of strength and balance, so it knows what you are capable of handling at any given moment. It's possible to overrule your subconscious—but only if you are conscious of what it's doing.

Far from being found wanting, you've handled your situation this way because of the caring, strong, giving, loving qualities you possess. Well, at least until you are pushed too far. (Then you don't become mean; you just think that's what has happened because you are so set in ways of peace, love, giving, and forgiving.)

Denial is a gift; it gives you the ability to shut off or minimize your awareness of threatening events; it saves you from being overwhelmed and made helpless, Bambi-Brain setting in where you can't function well or protect yourself adequately. Being overwhelmed creates helplessness, so your wired-in denial system opens a way for you focus on small portions of a problem at a time, and allows the massive, often smothering problem to fall out of your conscious thought completely at times. All this in service of survival of both mind and body. As you've seen here so far, the stress of thinking about and coping with things going on around you associated with your partner's drinking can have serious effects on your mental and emotional wellbeing, and have serious physical effects. Denial allows you a little more leeway, and you survive. You're not necessarily happy, but you survive because denial allows you to function even in the face of extreme pressures.

Denial, minimizing or dodging a problem, plays a large part in over-drinking and, as a result, has a bad name currently, but its intended purpose is quite beneficial. When it overrides a reality that can become life- or mind-threatening, it's very good. It's so good that it brings relief especially sweet to your subconscious—which makes denial a stronger tool for it to deal with your pressures.

When it allows you to escape mental anguish briefly, it is good. For example, when a loved one has died, a form of denial with numbing lets us make it through. No one can bear the wracking pain of losing a loved one continuously and deeply. Hence, denial. For survival.

You can see it's basically a protective brain function, parceling out your capacity to take in an overwhelming situation.

Most of you have never wanted to believe your guy was becoming a wreck, especially backing off from believing he could be unsalvageable. At this point in this book, you have learned that could possibly be the case. He may be a wreck, heading ever faster into absolute self-destruction, running right over everything that blocks his way. And you are learning that it's also possible that if he is diminished sufficiently (which happens much earlier than most people think) he has little hope of pulling out of it. Some hope, but very little.

Maybe you still love him, or maybe he is an important element of your own best survival interests.

You may more easily recognize denial working in you in times you've gotten just so far into thinking about or looking for a solution, and then thrown up your hands with Scarlet O'Hara's line: "I'm all out of steam and ideas here! I'll just drop it for now and worry about it tomorrow."

It can feel like a phantom gust of wind. Poof! and your mind jumps to something else. To keep the overwhelming thoughts at bay a part of you has to begin shutting down, even forgetting events or jumping back mentally when they come on because "they are just too much to deal with right now. I'll get to it later."

You know with your intelligent mind that just because you don't *want* to know something or think about something doesn't make it go away. But denial is subconscious, so it can play with magic.

Without conscious interference, it is capable of running the whole show—and its best trick is getting you focused on things outside the immediate catastrophe. And the relief is always welcome.

The coming checklist is going to get you back in reality, make a conscious intervention. And you'll be able to do this as you recognize that while the relief feels wonderful and taking the pressure off certainly helps you mentally and physically, not dealing with ugly problems can be deadly.

Psych Note: "Denial" is a full or partial closing of the mind to concrete thought about a threatening reality.

Is He Alcoholic?

This is the question most over-drinkers's women have. Most women who become drinkers's women (meaning they stay when others would have flown due to their extreme levels of compassion, generosity, caring, and love) resist labeling their mates as "alcoholic." Their denial systems begin pulling the shades the first time they read the short lists of signs, even when they recognized that he has them.

Knowing the truth of his condition is of primary importance to you, not only for your happiness and best interests, but for your emotional, mental, and physical survival.

Knowing the stage of a drinker's problem also makes it possible for professionals to tailor the form of treatment with the best chance of working for his specific stage. This approach, however, isn't being used in any current treatment approach that I've investigated to date. Nor has it been seen to be worth the expense of implementing to those who hold the treatment business purse-strings.

The questionnaire you'll be working with includes some items similar to those on other lists, but goes far, far beyond. Professionals currently are forced to use the existing guidelines, even though it is obvious they are part of the problem, the problem of why so few people recover from alcohol problems and stay recovered.

We licensed professionals cannot offer therapy that is not approved by the "rulers" of protocol, those who vote on and write our guide books for just what we are supposed to do for a given disorder. We cannot receive insurance payment for services unless the "patient" is diagnosed along these inadequate, ineffective lines. In fact, a professional can lose her licenses for not sticking with these old, inadequate, ineffective guidelines and methods in treating a patient.

Extending the diagnostic criteria, the list of signs of a drinking problem, to allow for earlier intervention is the primary reason I created this list of items in the first place, long before writing these books (due to my frustration with the ineffective status quo in addictions treatment.)

Very Real Brain Damage
Brain scans find holes in the brains of over-drinkers; how big the holes are varies mostly with how long they have been drinking. This factual element of assessment is not currently part of a primary diagnostic.

It's not a huge intellectual leap to start looking for additional diagnostic techniques and tools, in order to start getting treatment to drinkers before it has time to create such drastic damage. The checklist here includes such signs, those that show p long before those holes in the brain get so huge the sufferer hasn't enough brain power left to escape his dreadful consequence, to recover and stay that way.

Not surprisingly, a number of mental health practitioners tell me they are on board with expanding the list of signs that mark the deterioration of an over-drinker. They agree that using such a assessment guide will allow needed treatment far earlier in the destruction of his life. And the lives of those around him.

While no fixed "line" marks where a drinker changes from nice guy to horse's butt, we can allowing earlier diagnosis by an expanded tracking of deterioration serious drinkers have in common, thus saving lives—of drinkers and their partners.

Most people continue to hold the idea that until one is jobless, homeless, sick, weak, and disreputable he isn't "alcoholic," although the alcohol problem is off to a flying start in all people with their very first drink! And that is not due to the drinker's weak will; it's due to the action of alcohol on body and brain cells. For those with a genetic setup for it, this brain cell destruction accrues faster.

In truth, the potential for developing "alcoholism" commences at the very first drink. It all depends on the drinker's mental, emotional, and genetic set-up. Events and changes that occur as drinking gets worse also signal to some extend when the drinker is caught in the trap and sinking, the trap that fewer than 10 percent escape and remain free.

(The rest of the book also discusses the difficulty of a drinker's staying quit, explaining various physical complications that lead to breaking the will—and mind.)

While alcohol deadens, then kills, nerve cells (especially brain cells), that's not the worst of it. The worst of it is that the first and hardest hit brain cells happen to be in critical portions of the brain: the brain areas responsible for judgement, including judging whether he's had enough to drink! The decision-making area is affected accordingly, warping judgements like whether to put on the brakes now, or whether to shut up now, or refuse a drink. Bad judgement sounds like: "I'm not too drunk to drive.

Then there are the brain cells making up his memory: Short-term memory is located in one of the areas first hit by alcohol. Once he takes a drink, he forgets that he just decided he was going to quit. Perhaps more importantly, he forgets his reasons for not wanting to drink too much.

He forgets how many he's had so he's unsure when he reaches the limit he's set. He forgets how much his family means to him. He forgets his marriage vows.

As the alcohol load in his blood picks up, being disposed of far slower than it's being refilled, all brain cells slug down. First injured, numbed and slowed, then wounded, then dying—and no treatment known today restores a damaged or dead brain cell. The information each injured and dying brain cell holds evaporates. Even if brain cells did grow back, the replacements wouldn't hold the information encoded in the originals. Just growing new cells wouldn't give him access to earlier memories.

Memory: A promise to be home in time for dinner; remembering how bad a hangover feels; all of his vows never to do it again.

The coming checklist has so many signs listed, signs that are observable to almost anyone, but for sure most of it is observable by the woman who lives with him. Enough signs that it is impossible for a diagnostician to miss a developing drinking problem.

Research has shown that all of these signs accompany a progressing drinking problem. I wonder if there were so many signs of heart trouble or cancer, would a diagnostic guide for professionals leave off hundreds of other signs that could make a diagnosis clear.

I've made sure that the signs I've listed are observable, meaning that anyone could see them. (Of course, no one sees all of the action behind the scenes except those who live with him, so while anyone *could* see them, most are strenuously hidden by the drinker and rarely seen—until the bitter end—except by his mate. (Even she won't see it all, as most of you already know; over-drinkers are masters at hiding what they do. And why not? They truly believe they must have the elixir when they need it to survive; thus anything that could threaten that easy access is seen as "the enemy."

While some signs may not be *directly* observable by the drinker's woman, she usually knows about them, for instance, about other heavy drinkers in the family line, and about many of his early drinking escapades—how old he was, etc. (Again I point out: Doctors ask about heart problems and cancer in the family and use those to make their diagnoses of an individual. But not about drinking. Yet.)

(Note: As to heredity, the drinking problem sometimes "skips" generations, only to pop up again later. Like blue eyes or red hair. Someone once said that if "alcoholism" isn't hereditary, it must be contagious! That's because so many in families develop the same problem.)

Signs you'll see listed include those seen in the very Early Stage, usually, signs that are dismissed as "just part of drinking," or "just a young man sowing his oats."

Problem is: Millions of young men dabble, but they don't become fixated on doing more of it. Most likely, the chemicals in alcohol mimicking feel-good brain chemicals, certain genetic deficiencies or strangeness are involved in why some young men continue to become alcoholic and others don't.

If these problems are "just part of growing up," how do we explain billions of youths who don't go further?

Almost everyone believes that drinking "hard liquor" is worse than drinking beer or wine. Is that you? Take a look at this:

The Amount of Pure Alcohol in

a regular mixed drink: *1½ ounces of alcohol*

a 5-ounce glass of wine: *1½ ounces of alcohol*

an 8-ounce can of beer: *1½ ounces of alcohol*

If you don't know about the alcohol content in a drink, he'll fool you: "Ah, I just had a couple of beers."
And much of the world stays ignorant of the amount of alcohol, the chemical that makes you drunk, in various drinks.
You can see that two or three beers will have the same effect of two or three mixed drinks.
If a drinker shows differences, it's due to his system interacting with the additives to the alcohol and other factors.
But it's the alcohol content that makes him drunk.

For those who continue to drink more than the one to three drinks per 24 hours—known as over-drinking, drinking more than the highest amount considered safe by the National Institutes of Health—only trouble lies ahead. Yet it can be headed off years before the drinker has destroyed everything around him. That's why we must begin spotting it earlier. It's like catching a transmittable disease before it has a chance to destroy.

We have learned in all other health disorders, the sooner spotted, the more likely prevented and remedied. No physician finding a lump in your breast, no matter how small, fears he shouldn't diagnose sufficiently to allow for further testing. The physician doesn't decide that diagnosis should wait until the lump is a certain size, or crosses some "line" before taking it seriously.

Whether lumps, vascular irregularities, or signs of infection, physicians immediately set up further exams and discuss early intervention with the patient.

But not with over-drinking.

Most professionals can't know about (they're not published, taught, or given prescriptive therapy for) using the early signs of a problem destined for hell to help the patient. To do this, the partner's input, assessment, is far more reliable than anything the patient will say. Listen to him—but rather than buying in, concentrate on ways you can help him see his reality.

Making it harder for a physician or counselor to see the reality of an over-drinker is that even in an early stage, he's rarely going to tell the truth about how much he drinks for fear of being cut off from it.

Professionals must start relying on outside observations, interview the people close to the drinker in order to make a valid diagnosis. It's similar to the way we work with children. We get input about their behaviors from their parents, their teachers, other counselors who have been involved with him. This is the approach required to help the over-drinker.

> *The least reliable person in the world to accurately report the truth about his drinking is the drinker.*
>
> *The most reliable person for information about his drinking, especially the worst of it, is his mate. (But even she doesn't know all of it, the worst of it, because he hides it from her, and he'll likely try to hide it from the professional.)*

A physician is not concerned that a lump could turn out to be a false sign so she doesn't say anything or advise treatment! To the contrary, the physician hopes it will turn out to be nothing. (And the insurance company does too.)

Yet none of the disorders currently better treated causes the disruption and destruction of the lives of everyone the patient touches like over-drinking. Most professionals continue to hold back saying what needs to be said out of fear of error, or losing a patient—as well as having the cultural vague sense of having no right to pry into someone's drinking. Professionals! Get over it!

Numerous books have been written for and about the caretakers of chronically ill persons—all with a strong focus on how the stress of their relationship with the impaired person affects them. But no such book has been written for the partners of an over-drinker. Well, until now.

I hope that this chapter and its questionnaire give you the information you need for your future interactions with him. You, the drinker's woman, are likely the only person on earth who sees those early signs—(and a great many of those that follow). You may already have experienced resistance getting friends and family (his family mostly) to see that he has a problem. Sometimes his family and friends point to you as the problem. I mean, what else could they think: It's what he tells them (and they do see you—stressed, angry, maybe edgy. Even when his problem and its consequent behaviors become blatant, many remain in denial. "It's really not that bad." (Meaning: "The lump doesn't yet weight a full pound so ignore it!")

All questions on the coming checklist address signs of over-drinking that anyone very close to the drinker can see. The drinker, however, allows fewer and fewer people that close. On their own, a sign may mean little, but when they appear together, there's a problem—current or in the making. I listed the many signs roughly in the order they *usually* occur. While not all drinkers do all the listed things, or in precisely in the same order, all over-drinkers will do most of these things in roughly the same order. That's because alcohol damages brain cells the same way in most people. Brain cells change or die in the same brain areas, producing nearly the same behaviors in over-drinkers. Like tuberculosis, where the same kind of damage occurs in the same organ of people who have it, with about the same result. Death, if not treated adequately.

Some drinkers can skip chunks of signs on this list, jumping from Early Middle Stage signs straight into

23

End Stage signs, hence, when you come to a string of items that seem not to apply, don't stop there. Continue assessing items to the very end. Some drinkers anchor at a level, maybe for years, before observable changes start appearing again.

There is a second reason for continuing on down the list of signs. Because brain damage causes behavioral change the same in all over-drinkers, looking at signs further along shows you what to expect. Knowing what's coming also tunes your subconscious to pick up on them when they begin occurring. You won't miss them.

It is possible for an over-drinker to leap over some markers of downfall and rush far ahead into more advanced levels.

This most often occurs when something especially bad happens to him—getting a terminal disease, death of a loved one, loss of a job or career, financial ruin, or other such tragedies. He's already drinking (and already has a problem in the cooker), but because alcohol brings mental and emotional relief (temporarily), he will turn to it, and step it up. This is why many people think it was the bad event that caused his problem—but he already had the problem before the bad event. The bad event simply speeded up his deterioration.

An over-drinker "knows" how to relieve his mental discomfort-and emotional pain. Drinkers who have held the line for a long time will seek that relief more often after an unhappiness. His drinking picks up, his deterioration takes him down.

Many drinkers's women say that they feel guilty for not really caring a lot if he gets injured or commits suicide. In fact, many admit to flashes of maybe being relieved should it happen. Who can blame them? I ask you: Is it bad to wish the guy firing cannon balls at you would drop dead? No, of course not. Those feelings are actually normal! They prove you are normal. Drop any guilty feelings.

Attention!

An over-drinker drinks for only one reason: The feeling it gives him.

He doesn't drink because he had a hard day, or because you were mean to him. He drinks because when things happen that he doesn't like and make him feel bad, he has discovered a way to change that— fast. His subconscious took over from there. It works the same with chocolate cake, smoking, drugs, gambling, sexual adventures (sounds fun when I say it like that!), with prescription and other drugs.

His dependence on this way of getting relief, coupled with specific cells of his body actually becoming dependent on a goodly supply of alcohol add up to addiction in its fullest form. Body cells must adjust to large amounts of alcohol when drinking picks up; they must change their makeup to cope. When the alcohol stops, they are in distress because they have changed to function with it. Without it, they don't work well. This, combined with the actual poisoning of his body with over-drinking are what's going on when he has a hangover.

When his intake of alcohol stops, every cell in his body begins will cry out for it. Having altered themselves over time, these cells growing a little here, shrinking a little there, producing less of whatever the cell produces because the alcohol begins takes its place in the . The cell has adjusted to accommodate loads of alcohol, and like a balloon that has been stretched too far now hangs slack and useless because they now need alcohol to function.

These body cells set up an inner scream like nothing else can, blocking most other thought.

* * *

Ready, Set? . . .

Okay—make your trip to the bathroom, get some coffee or tea or whatever works for you, and find a quiet space where you can work for the next hour or so without interruption. (It's not the end of the world if you get interrupted; it just means you have to hunker down later to regain your level of concentration.)

Now, with pencil in hand, read each item, each one a sign commonly seen in problem drinkers. Not all signs will appear in all drinkers, and not all will appear in exactly the same order. If you have observed a sign in your drinker (or know it is fact) put a checkmark by it.

The checklist is for you—not a judge, not the evening news. You can share it later if you wish, especially with his physician, but its purpose is just for you to get an idea of what's going on with him, for you to diagnose (roughly) how far the problem that is ripping your life apart has progressed.

Relax as you answer the questions. You aren't swearing to your answers in a court of law!

Now will missing a few, or checking a few incorrectly won't make a big difference in your final outcome.

PRE-DRINKING
SPOTTING THE SET-UP

(His Physical and Genetic situation that can set him up for developing problems with alcohol

____1. Did (do) either of his parents drink too much?

____2. Did (do) any of his siblings drink too much?

____3. Did (do) any of his grandparents drink too much?

____4. Did (do) any of his great-grandparents drink too much?

____5. Did (do) any of his blood-related aunts or uncles drink too much?

____6. Is he over 40 years old?

____7. Is he under 24 years old? (Age 24 is approximately when the brain stops growing. Until then, it's is still growing, thus susceptible to far more damage than it will a few years later.)

*   *   *

STAGE ONE

FIRST STAGE
(Even if your guy is beyond the early stages and no longer does these things, if he did them in the past, check them.)

The Early First Stage

____8. Is there a change in his personality when drinking?

____9. Does (or did) he seem to "hold his liquor" better than others do in the early days?

____10. Does he drink fast?

____11. Does he appear to look forward to drinking events?

____12. Does he talk about drinking as if it's a lot of fun?

____13. Does he enjoy leisure activities less where he can't include drinking?

(A thought to contemplate: If you've seen him drink an entire six-pack, think: Does he ever sit down and drink a six-pack of spring water? Or cola?)

____14. Does he act grandiose when drinking?

____15. When he drinks, does he drink more than the U.S. National Institutes of Health says is the safe amount?

____16. Does he drink more than others with him?

____17. When most others quit, does he continue?

____18. Does (did) his sex drive increase when drinking early on?

_____19. Has anyone ever said "He seems to have a hollow leg"?

_____20. Does he drink until he gets drunk?

_____21. Is he moody, depressed, easily angered, jumpy, or sick after drinking the night before?

_____22. Does he go on to drink again after suffering for it (either a bad hangover or some other negative experience that was connected to his drinking)?

_____23. Has he ever appeared not to remember any part of his drinking time?

The Mid-First Stage

(Be sure to take note of the first item of each stage; that item is the sign moving him up from one level to the next.)

_____24. Did he go back and drink again, continue to drink (and over-drink) after experiencing bad events associated with his drinking?

_____25. Do certain events (or feelings) seem to trigger him to think about getting a drink?

_____26. Does he use excuses to drink (and over-drink) like "I had a bad day," or "It's the President's birthday" ?

_____27. Has he become more critical of others?

_____28. Does he seem to look forward to getting a drink, as if it is a party or a reward? (Like at the end of a work day or his work week.)

_____29. Does he seem to look forward to social gatherings where there will be drinking?

_____30. Does he appear uncomfortable if he cannot drink at social gatherings?

_____31. Has his behavior when drinking ever embarrassed you?

_____32. Does (or did) he do foolish or dangerous things when drinking?

_____33. When fixing drinks, does he sneak an extra pop, or a whole drink?

_____34. Is he more boisterous when drinking?

_____35. Does he drink more in amount now than in the past?

_____36. Does he drink more often now than in the past?

_____37. Does he buy more alcohol now than in the past?

_____38. Does he neglect food, or eat less, when drinking?

_____39. Have you complained about things that he does while he's drinking?

The Late First Stage
(Again—note the first item, the signal he's moved deeper.)

_____40. Did the behaviors you complained about continue to be a problem?

_____41. Or did they stop for a while, but then come back?

_____42. Have you complained to him about how much he drinks, or how often?

_____43. After you complained, did he try to cut down or quit?

_____44. Did he get irritable because you complained?

_____45. Did he continue to drink anyway or, if he decided to cut down or quit, did he eventually go back to it?

_____46. Has he ever excused something he did by saying, "I only did that because I was drunk"? (This item shows that he loses control when drinking, otherwise he wouldn't do something drinking that he would not do otherwise.)

_____47. Has he ever changed his routine to have more opportunities for drinking? (Like getting together with friends or joining a new group of friends.)

_____48. Does he act uncomfortable (or disturbed) when you talk to him about his drinking?

_____49. Has he said he wanted a drink to relax, unwind, chill, loosen up, forget the bad day or event? (Drinking to get a specific feeling. Saying it shows he knows it's unusual.)

_____50. Has he said any of those things more than once?

_____51. Is he having money problems, yet he continues to spend money on drinking?

_____52. Does he drink to calm down when upset?

_____53. When talking about drinking, does he say "I'm going to have a drink," when he'll surely have more than one?

____54. Has he ever planned or promised to drink only a certain amount, then went ahead and had more than that amount? (This is a sign of loss of control.)

____55. Has he ever planned not to drink at all at some event, then did anyway?

____56. Has he ever failed to keep a commitment due to something associated with his drinking?

____57. Has he said he doesn't want to drink before a specific time of day?

____58. Has he tried to cut down on his drinking on his own?

____59. Did his attempt to cut down eventually fail?

____60. Has he said he felt badly about his drinking, or things he had done when drinking?

*   *   *

STAGE TWO
MIDDLE STAGES

The Early Middle Stage
(Again, note the item marking his step-up to a more serious stage.)

____61. Having said that he feels bad about his behavior when he was drinking, did he then go on to drink again?

____62. Has he ever been drinking (or over-drinking) at an inappropriate time?

____63. Has he become more critical of others (including you), even when not drinking?

____64. Does he often dodge his responsibility for when bad things happen (especially those occurring when he was drinking)? (Usually this happens by his blaming others.)

____65. Is he evasive about how much, how often, with whom, where, or other information about his drinking?

____66. Is drinking interfering with his hobbies or sports so that he's doing less of things he used to enjoy?

____67. Has he made you give excuses to anyone for his behavior, or his absences, due to over-drinking?

____68. Has he made a rule to do most of his drinking at home?

____69. Did he eventually break his own rule?

____70. Has he promised to drink less at home, but eventually started drinking as much again?

____71. When you confronted him about drinking more, did he start drinking more often away from home? (Where his behavior couldn't be tracked as well by your lying eyes?)

____72. Has he become upset when prevented from going to a drinking event?

____73. Does he avoid family members who don't drink?

____74. Does he avoid friends who don't drink?

_____75. Does he select mostly entertainment that allows drinking?

_____76. As a couple, do you not associate with friends as much anymore because of his drinking, or his behavior?

_____77. Has he lied to anyone about his drinking?

_____78. Has he begun staying out later drinking?

_____79. Has he changed the type of drinks he drinks (such as from liquor to beer, or beer to light beer) in an attempt to cut down his drinking?

_____80. Does he get defensive or argumentative if someone other than you talks to him about his drinking?

_____81. Do friends say that they think he's drinking too much?

_____82. Has his spending associated with drinking (or drinking behavior) begun to drain the family?

_____83. Has he become more self-centered?

_____84. Does he speak of wanting to "get drunk"?

_____85. Have you ever spoken to a family member about your concerns over his drinking?

_____86. Does he drink when angry?

_____87. Does he often seem unable to remember everything that happened while he was drinking?

_____88. Has he ever asked someone what happened during any of the time he was drinking?

_____89. Has he, when drinking, ever hurt your feelings (or other people's)?

_____90. Has he promised not to do it again, but then has done it again when drinking?

_____91. Has he ever tried to quit drinking?

The Mid-Middle Stage
(Note the first item. It signals another step down.)

____91. Did his attempt to quit drinking fail?

____92. Has he begun to lose interest in things he used to enjoy?

____93. Has he become more aggressive when drinking or hung-over?

____94. Has his behavior embarrassed you?

____95. Has he started arguments with you while drinking?

____96. Has he started arguments with others when drinking?

____97. Have you talked to one of your friends about his drinking?

____98. Does he drink when others do not?

____99. Is his drinking causing other problems in the home?

____100. Has he neglected an obligation—work, family, health, job, or appointments—due to drinking or something associated with his drinking?

____101. Has he missed an important appointment or event due to drinking or something associated with drinking?

____102. Has he hidden or lied to you about his drinking, especially concerning the amount?

____103. Does he become more restless when he's not drinking?

____104. Has he said that a drink helps him get away from pressures for a while? (Changing his feelings.)

_____105. Has he ever mentioned wondering if he had a drinking problem?

_____106. Does he spend a lot of time drinking?

_____107. Has he ever set a limit on how much to drink at home or an event, or any other time?

_____108. Has he gone beyond a limit he set? (Sign of inability to control his drinking.)

_____109. Does he hurt you emotionally or become verbally abusive when he is drinking?

_____110. Has he left an argument with you to get a drink or go out drinking?

_____111. Has he ever been in trouble with his job or work due to something associated with drinking?

_____112. Does he plan things but not follow through (more than in the past)?

_____113. Does he start on projects, then drop them (more than in the past)?

_____114. Are you unsure about how much he's drinking now?

_____115. Has he taken up a hobby/sport to help him cut down on his drinking?

_____115. Did that attempt eventually fail?

_____116. Has he changed his usual drink to boost the kick? Or use drugs, legal or illegal, to do that?

_____117. Has he changed his type of alcoholic drink to help him cut down and control his drinking?

_____118. Has that tactic failed to help him cut down (and stay cut down)? (The beginning of loss of control.)

_____119. Does he get into arguments with others in social settings, such as at parties?

_____120. Has he lost friends due to his drinking?

_____121. Has he kept a "stash" of alcohol in a place where he could get a drink secretly?

_____122. Have family members asked you to get him to cut down or to quit?

_____123. Has he ever seen a list of signs of a drinking problem and been argumentative or sarcastic about them?

_____124. Has he recognized that he has signs of a problem, but continued drinking?

_____125. Does he drink when bored?

_____126. Has he changed his routine to help him cut down his drinking?

_____127. Have his changes eventually failed to work?

_____128. Has he made more than one serious attempt to quit?

_____129. Did these attempts fail?

_____130. Has he left a specific group of people in an attempt to cut down on his drinking?

_____131. Did it fail to keep him cut down-quit?

_____132. Have you ever found liquor he'd watered down to make the bottle appear fuller, or a totally replaced a bottle for the same reason?

_____133. Has he been in physical fights when drinking?

_____134. When he controls his drinking for some special occasion, does he soon afterward drink more?

_____135. Has there been more than one time he confessed to bad behavior, or expressed remorse for his behavior while drinking?

_____136. Was his expression of guilt or remorse completely believable?

_____137. Did he go back to drink again?

_____138. Has he ever left a job in order to cut down or quit drinking?

_____139. Did that change eventually fail?

_____140. Has he ever moved to another neighborhood or town in an attempt to get a new start, to cut down or quit drinking?

_____141. Did that attempt eventually fail?

_____142. Have you suspected that your drinker sets up arguments just to get an excuse to go drinking?

Late Middle Stage

_____143. Does he drink when he's alone?

_____144. Does he take one or two drinks fast, to get started?

_____145. Has he ever been arrested for anything associated with drinking?

_____146. Has he continued to drink after the arrest?

_____147. Has he suffered illness because of drinking?

_____148. Has he continued to drink even so?

_____149. Do you believe he is dependent on alcohol?

_____150. Has his physical health continued to deteriorate?

_____151. Have you suspected he was lying when he claimed no memory of something done while drinking?

_____152. Does he seem to have less fun when drinking now than in the past?

_____153. Has his personality changed even when he's not drinking?

_____154. Do you see physical signs of heavy drinking— broken veins, bloodshot eyes, looking tired or older, a swollen upper belly, slackened muscles?

_____155. Has he ever gone off a medication, or decided not to take a medication, because he could not drink alcohol while taking it?

_____156. Does he have decreased sex drive (or ability)?

_____157. Does he seem bored (or restless) more than in the past?

_____158. Has he—who never harmed or threatened you or your children before--when drinking threatened or committed such harm?

_____159. Has he threatened you more than once?

_____160. Has he threatened to harm you when he was not drinking?

_____161. Has he ever hurt you physically, or been violent with you?

If you answered "yes" to the last question, it is extremely important for you to seek qualified professional help as soon as possible, and certainly before trying to discuss any of this with him: A women's hotline counselor is your best bet, but a licensed mental health counselor, licensed social worker, or your health professional all can give you information to help keep you safe or set you up with others who can. If he has ever been violent, get direction from the professionals before talking to him about what you find. Also, keep in mind that there's really no need to talk to him about it. This man may be far beyond fixing with a talk.

You absolutely are not safe if you live with a problem drinker who ever becomes in the least violent. His behavior control is steadily slipping. This means you cannot predict when it will fail completely.

Staying free of crippling injuries, or losing your life—whether he meant to do it or not—depends on being aware, staying observant, and getting a qualified professional to guide you from here.

____162. Is his over-all physical condition continuing to deteriorate?

____163. Does he spend more time alone?

____164. Has he started drinking with people considered of a lower class than him?

____165. Does he flirt with other women while drinking?

____166. Have his morals slipped in other ways?

____167. Does he frequently talk about or show an excess of worry or fear?

____168. Has he begun having vision problems— especially night vision? (Alcohol can affect vision.)

____169. Does he seem to have long periods during drinking that he can't remember?

____170. Have other family members shown concern about his drinking?

____171. Does he blame others for his problems or for his over-drinking?

____172. Has he become almost continually critical of others?

____173. Has he ever made a show of leaving a little of his drink unfinished? (What normal drinker would do that?)

____174. Has he continued drinking all night?

____175. Has he begun to suffer high levels of anxiety or panic attacks, or spells of deep depression?

____176. Does he ever drink early in his day--before noon (or the equivalent if on shift work)?

____177. Does he drink the morning after over-drinking?

____178. Does he take a drink to ease a hangover?

____179. Has he become more jealous?

____180. Do you suspect him of sexual misbehavior?

____181. Have you suspected (or known) that your drinker has been sexually unfaithful?

____182. Does he appear to have memory problems even when not drinking?

____183. Has he ever drunk while on the job?

____184. Has he threatened to find somebody else (another woman) who understands him?

____185. Has he ever lost a job because of anything associated with his drinking?

____186. Has his job or other important source of his welfare suggested that he go for counseling?

____187. Has he gone for any type of counseling—or mental health treatment?

____188. Did he drop or discontinue treatment?

_____188. Has he told you (or do you suspect) that when he saw a counselor or doctor, he was not honest about his drinking?

_____189. Has he begun taking medication for anxiety, or sleep medications? (Anxiety and sleep disorder accompany a growing drinking problem.)

_____190. Has anyone ever called the police on him when he was drinking—even if he was innocent of the charge.

_____191. Has he continued drinking despite that?

_____192. Has he stopped or lessened expressing remorse for bad behavior?

_____193. Does he become verbally abusive (or shut you out completely) when you talk about his drinking?

_____194. Has he ever been injured seriously enough to require medical care associated with his drinking?

_____195. Has he been hospitalized due to drinking or something associated with his drinking?

_____196. Did he return to drinking after that?

_____197. Does he seem antsy when wanting to get a drink?

_____198. Is he having flashes of intense emotion— especially anger, fear, or jealousy—whether drinking or not?

_____199. Has he had an automobile accident when drinking or hung-over?

_____200. Has he ever been the driver, while drinking or hung-over, when someone else was injured?

_____201. After that accident, did he resume drinking at the same rate as before?

____203. Has he ever been arrested, or taken to jail for something associated with drinking?

____204. After getting out of jail, did he resume drinking?

____205. Have you seen signs of further diminishing health—he's paler, thinning hair, sexual problems, wasting away or packing on fat, broken veins on his face, easy bruising?

____206. Does he react with anger to your pointing out his health effects (perhaps going for a drink afterward)?

____207. Has he argued or become hostile when anyone else has tried to talk to him about his drinking, behavior, or health?

_☐_208. Have you begun to seek help for either him or yourself? (I checked this one for you. You're doing that by reading this book.)

____209. Have you spoken to a counselor or doctor about your partner's drinking?

____210. Has he ever been charged with drunk driving?

____211. After that charge, did he eventually resume drinking?

____212. Has he ever been open, even briefly, to getting any kind of help for the drinking?

____213. Does he seem to have frequent bouts of remorse?

____214. Does he have more than one hidden alcohol stash?

____215. Has he occasionally shown signs of wanting to get back into church, or other signs of spiritual hunger?

_____216. Has your partner ever gone to a counselor, physician, or minister specifically for help with his drinking?

_____217. Has he ever been in jail overnight or longer for something associated with drinking (different from just going to jail and bonding out)?

_____218. Did he continue drinking after that?

_____219. Has he ever attended a meeting of Alcoholics Anonymous?

_____220. Does he ever say he hates himself?

_____221. Have his testicles or penis shrunk? (BTW-- Over-drinking causes male genitals to shrink, often first seen in his testicles.)

* * *

STAGE FOUR

END STAGE

_____222. Has he ever been hospitalized for mental health or substance abuse treatment?

_____223. After treatment, did he eventually start drinking?

_____224. He's used up his excuses for over-drinking; he no longer gives excuses when he drinks.

_____225. Have almost all family and friends backed away from him?

_____226. Does he continue to drink, despite illnesses or health warnings?

____227. Has he sought out spiritual help, but it failed to stop the drinking (for good)?

____228. Has he stopped making plans to do anything?

____229. Do his hands shake, especially early in his day?

____230. Do you notice tremors in his hands, voice, even his knees, when he's not drinking?

____231. Have you noticed that shakes diminish or disappear for a while after he takes a drink?

____232. Does he ever appear unsteady when walking, even when not drinking?

____233. Does he spend most of his time (off work) isolated and drinking (at home or in a favorite bar)?

____234. Has he committed a felony when drinking?

____235. Has he served a jail/prison sentence?

____236. Has he continued drinking after that?

____237. Does he have any type of liver trouble?

____238. Does he have any pancreas trouble?

____239. Has he ever vomited blood (dark red or bright red)?

____240. Does he continue to drink despite serious health issues?

____241. Does he have difficulty sleeping—unable to asleep for more than a few hours at a time?

____242. Does he get up and drink to get back to sleep?

____243. Does he have a swollen, hard upper belly?

____244. Is he drinking less alcohol at a sitting now, but he still seems to get drunk?

_____245. Does he have an illness that can kill him if he continues drinking?

_____246. Does he continue to drink even so?

_____247. Has he made more than one attempt at getting help?

_____248. Did he return to drinking?

_____249. Has he said he-others would be better off if he were dead?

_____250. Has he ever threatened suicide?

_____251. Has he been hospitalized for any illness associated with or aggravated by his drinking?

_____252. Did he start drinking again after that?

_____253. Does he seem to have given up on changing?

_____254. Has he ever said he doesn't care if something kills him—like an accident, his health, the drinking?

_____255. Has he ever said he hopes something kills him?

_____256. Has he attempted to kill himself?

_____257. Has he attempted to kill someone else—even if he says he wasn't serious (or was "just drunk")?

_____258. Has he become vegetative, sitting or sleeping much of the time if not working?

_____259. Is he frequently incoherent or impossible to talk to because he's drunk?

_____261. Did he actually commit suicide? Or has he died of other causes associated with his drinking?

Okay. That's it! You're done.

And you've done well to get here. Good Girl!

(Pat yourself on the butt and say, "Good Girl!" to yourself.)

Now What?

You have a lot of factual material to work with now, certainly more than you did when you picked up this book.

No matter what you discover on this checklist, you are bound to have millions (many millions!) of sisters in the United States alone whose drinkers are in more or less the same stages. That means they will be going through more or less the same things you are dealing with. Again--you are not alone! I guarantee you that all of you can be of great help to one another, which is the reason for our blog.

This is a great time to take a short break—even overnight, let all this information begin to settle in. Or—you can keep right on! It's your decision.

* * *

What Does This Check-List Tell You?

Having this questionnaire to work with means that you don't need a professional to diagnose him and know what's going on. You may, however, need a professional or a trained women's hotline counselor to help you decide what's best and safest for you to do about it, given your current circumstances.

The behaviors that you just examined are all signs that would be observable to anyone—especially anyone as close to the drinker as you are. (As you've likely also observed, over-drinkers are very clever at hiding their true condition from others.)

Let's see what you see. Based on your checkmarks, answer these questions:

Do you think he has a drinking problem?

_____

If so, what stage is indicated?

_____

What events does your checklist suggest likely come next on his way down?

1. _____

2. _____

3. _____

How do you feel about what likely comes next?

_____

_____

*   *   *

You have absorbed a load of information now, mostly information I know you were looking for—but didn't necessarily want. Others have used what they learned up to this point to understand their drinker's situation, and better understand their own position. They and you are better informed, more likely to make your best decisions with the knowledge you have gained.

Understand that it is without doubt the "vested interests" that have allowed the general culture to misunderstand drinking. Think how much money is spent on just television ads to get people to drink, and drink more. For them, it's business; we don't condemn the makers and suppliers of alcohol. We do condemn their failure to inform the consumers. Alcohol has been around since the first people, and it is fine—when used with full knowledge of its properties and their effects. If the facts here were widely known, especially if they were taught in health classes before middle-school age, the businesses would still make billions—and the population would save billions on damage and "treatment," etc.

The way things are and have been make it appear that the businesses have used this information to do what's best for them—**not the consumer (and his family).**

Many of your rare and beautiful sisters have based their life decisions at this point back on the dream or wish that the drinker will get better. Also on the belief they really can change another person *and make them stay changed.*

I hope that every one of you who want to remain in your relationship or in your home will be able to do so. The information and tricks here will be a big help. The information you've gained this far puts you in a much better position to consider your future paths, to consider and weigh out your own best interests, to make the best decision you can at that moment (which is truly the best anyone can ever do).

Making any decision or change at this point will likely be difficult, likely painful. And you may find out as you try to follow through that you're not able to—at least not immediately. Not doing anything is also painful; I would say not doing anything can be more painful. Making a decision doesn't cure the problem; it only gives you a focus that will like take you closer to your cure, step by step..

If you can help the drinker without sacrificing yourself, by all means do so. Be watchful *not* to sacrifice your own best interests in the hope your sacrifice will work. It won't. Look at the record. Backing up a step here leaves you less to bargain with later too.

Both your conscious and subconscious mind(s) will continue processing all the things you have taken in. Bit by bit it will fall in place to soon seem natural and normal. This means you can relax now and let things fall into place as they do; let up any push—unless your situation is dangerous. Don't try to force anything if you don't have to for safety's sake.

Get busy, get active—do something, preferably something enjoyable as you mull these things over for a few days. Relax into your daily processes while your subconscious slowly sorts out the pieces.

*   *   *

I Remember . . . My Fear of Losing Him

I remember being afraid to let go of him, even though he had become a monster, who hit me and ran around on me—to name only a few problems. I just knew that if I let go some other woman would swoop him up, and that he'd then settle down and become a sweet and wonderful guy. I was afraid that he'd finally control his drinking, make a wonderful home for her, and I would have lost him—this incredible man—forever.

Well, in the twenty years since, I've discovered that not a single one of the undisclosed number of men I had loved and left had changed—those I knew of were still Horse's Butts. Or dead. Certainly none of them had changed enough that I could bear seeing them again, much less live with them. Oh, by the way—their lack of change was true even with all those new partners.

I Also Remember . . .

A couple of years ago (some 50 years after my divorce from him), an ex-husband, father of my four sons, called me—out of the blue. Hadn't heard from him in 30 years—and had never received even a dollar in child support from him.

Because this man had been extremely violent, I long ago determined to avoid any contact with him and gladly sacrificed the pittance he would have paid for child support to hide from and avoid him. Nevertheless, when he called I was curious on the chance he was calling about something important to do with the boys, so I didn't hang up immediately, my reflex response.

"Why are you calling me?" I said, with no friendly tone.

"Oh, there's no problem," he said. "I'm just checking up to see how you are doing."

"Huh," I said. I was surprised, shocked, and in the clutches of a minor Brain Freeze because of it.

"I'm rather busy and need to Move Along," I finally said.

"I just wanted to talk about the old times," he said, the nice guy plea in his voice, a tone that I remembered well although it had been nearly 50 years since I had heard it.

I'm sure my next words sprang from years of practice because they came automatically. I was getting practice through the years too every time I coached a woman on memorizing and using similar words:

"Bubba (we're Southern remember), I really don't want to talk with you. If I liked you at all, I'd probably still be married to you. I don't want to talk to you and I don't want you ever to call me again."

"But baby," he came back, with that same old wounded puppy whine in his voice, "what's wrong with talking? We're both older now, it's all in the past, why can't we just talk? I just wanted to talk about all the good times we had together."

I was dumbfounded. Speechless.

What did he just say? "All the good times"?

The surprise and perhaps a tinge of rage created a lot of energy to bolster my reply. I became extremely assertive (well, perhaps a bit aggressive) when I reflexively said, "Good times? Are you nuts? What do you mean 'good times'? I don't remember any good times!

"I do remember that you cheated on me so many times that I can't remember how many. I do remember that you lied to me even more times. I remember that you wouldn't work, that you took all the money that I made. I remember how awful you talked to me, the names you called me, the hateful things you said to me and told other people about me. And I remember that you hit me—a lot, and sometimes beat me horribly. I remember . . . ." And now he was shouting, interrupting me.

"See how you are?" his voice now nasal, strident. The old blaming tone I also remembered so well.

Then he launched the attack (his old trick that used to cower me because I felt so inadequate, and so aware of the power of his fists.)

"You know," he said then, with more stridency, "this is what was always wrong with you!" A breath: "You're so negative!"

I was flabbergasted, but only for a moment. Because of years of learning and practicing assertiveness, developing a lovely self-esteem and a sense of my goodness and value, as well as a lot of self-confidence, I blurted out, "Good-bye. Don't **ever** call me again." Click.

(Later, my youngest son told me his dad had called him and asked what in the world was wrong with his mother. He complained that I had been

nasty to him! Can you believe it! Oh, yeah—I forgot—
you can.)

This man, who, all those years ago I was so afraid
to let go of because he might change—turn it all
around and become wonderful and I'd miss out on
it—had not changed one whit in the nearly half-
century since then.

He still used the old switch-and-attack tricks that
he used back then, when they worked so well for him.

More proof that he had not changed is the fact
that he called me at all. After all these years (and
several additional marriages that also failed for the
same reasons ours did) he was still in total denial of
his bad behavior.

Don't even think of pointing out the harm he
inflicted on me (and his four sons) in the doing, he
was still jumping up to blame me for the problem!

Sheesh.

So much for my fear of losing him because he
might change and become wonderful and some other
woman would get all that good stuff! Hah!

* * *

Another Kind of Story

A couple of buddies, Tom and Chet, over-drinkers both—finally found recovery after many, many tries.

Their drinking buddy George didn't make it though. He continued to drink and deteriorate.

The first couple of years, Tom and Chet tried to get George to come with them to the recovery program that was working so well for them, but he staunchly refused. "I don't need that!" he'd say, "I'm not that bad."

His life being unattractive to his friends, and theirs to him, they soon drifted apart.

About a year later, Chet saw George's obituary in the paper. Dismayed, he called Tom. They went sadly to the funeral home, where they found out that George had died of liver failure (the most common killer of over-drinkers who don't kill themselves in accidents or suicide before the liver goes).

They determined (correctly) that Chet's drinking had killed him and they felt really bad about it.

The next day, after the funeral service, Tom and Chet offered their sympathy to George's wife. They told her that George had been a good friend and asked if there was anything they could do to help her. She said no.

Then Tom asked if George had ever gone into any kind of alcohol treatment.

Aghast, George's wife drew back and, looking down her nose at them, said, "What do you mean? He wasn't *that* bad!"

Hmm.

He wasn't *that* bad?
He was only dead!

This, my lovelies, is a superb example of that thing we will call "partner denial."

* * *

We're done—for now. I'd love it if you read the entire book this chapter is taken from, *Does He Drink Too Much?*

We'd also love to see you and hear from you, what you're thinking, sharing your experiences to help other women, getting answers to any other questions you have, and seeing for yourself that you are not alone in the terrible trap that has caught him, yet severely affects you. It's like a fox getting caught in a trap and his mate, back at the cave, howling in pain. And most people just don't understand. Perhaps you can begin to fix that!

Tune in with us on our blog:
www.hedrinkstoomuch.com